The Mirror Hurlers

First published in 2020
Published by Puncher and Wattmann
PO Box 279
Waratah NSW 2298

http://www.puncherandwattmann.com
puncherandwattmann@bigpond.com

NATIONAL
LIBRARY
OF AUSTRALIA

A catalogue record for this book is available from the National Library of Australia

ISBN   9781922186966

Cover design by Miranda Douglas

Printed by Lightning Source International

This project has been assisted by the Australian Government through the Australia Council, its arts funding and advisory body.

Australian Government

Australia Council
for the Art

The Mirror Hurlers

Ross Gillett

PUNCHER & WATTMANN

For Julie

Contents

3

Brushcutter

Whatever he was saying went unheard
when at last it started with a vengeance.
Against its sudden high pitched yell, its frenzied
rattle, even his raised voice stood no chance.
He'd talked me through the late spring ritual,
telling me bush block stories as he wiped
the temperamental spark plug, mixed the fuel.
He fitted gleaming blades, and then he stooped
to start the thing. It yielded a dead cough.
He tinkered, tried again, until we heard
its promising little petrol-driven laugh.
He gave it quick full throttle and it roared.
I see my father frowning as he shouted
something at close range I never caught.

Braille

It's a father and daughter tour
and we stop for some cliffs.
A mountain valley running to the west,
waterfalls on a near rock face.

Ten years old,
she rests her chin on the railings to look.
I find a plaque that gives us
brief biographies of trees,
the local wind-resistant scrub.
It names names: that far peak,
the wrecked escarpment to the north.

Then the barely noticeable braille
punched out across the bottom of the sign
claims her attention. It's a rough
text she has never met,
stairways and doors of dots
the same dark blue as the background.

I explain. Eyes closed,
she lets her fingers move across
this touchable translation.
She opens her eyes and scans
the view again, almost as if − I can tell −
she has never looked that hard before.

Scoops of cliff, the horizon
with its worn ridges, a squall
approaching up the valley.

I watch her watching,
asking herself how she could ever see
these sharp-edged sweeps of land
through her fingertips. We are both
lost in the same wondering.

Along the walking track
my daughter feels the braille with both hands
whenever we find it footnoting
the smoothness of painted print.
She seems to be playing a small piano.
She does not watch the keyboard.

She is looking blindly into the sky
when the forgotten squall
arrives with a wind shift.

For a moment
we are caught in the open,
imagining the dark
possible world around us.
Rain beginning to read our faces.

Dancing with a Broken Belt

I knew I'd get the ruler
if both hands didn't meet above my head when they were meant to
which was what folk dancing seemed to be mainly about

so when the frayed belt snapped in the middle of a jig
and my knee length shorts began to sag
and my obedient arms raised themselves like the Pope's hat

I drew the attention of the suspicious teacher
by putting into practice a theory I have since applied to life generally
and which as often as not completely fails to prove correct

if you move your legs fast enough your pants will stay up

On Being a Man

For one thing
I have the strongest hands in the house.
My wife and children
try to turn off a dripping tap
and my teenage son can almost do it
but only I can twist with a grip
hard enough to stop that leak in its tracks
for another night
which means another day
I don't have to call in the plumber
who is even more of a man than I am.

The Wagon Train Lampshade

My parents went to America.
They came back with bits of the Wild West
just for me. The six shooter with an ivory handle,
the headdress thick with feathers.
I went to war with myself in style.

At night, their slide show kept me quiet.
Our lounge room wall was deep with scenes
I couldn't believe. A real chief
planting his hand on my father's shoulder,
a giant cactus standing over my mother.

When I went to bed, their best present
waited for me. A wagon train
blazed into being when I turned the lamp on.
Canopies like bonnets, big rickety wheels,
glowing horses in a frozen gallop.

And there in the distance, Indians
swooping out of the incandescence
at the heart of everything. I squinted
persistently into that brightness.
Rifles and riders were etched in light.

But my wayfaring mother would lean
hurriedly over me, deliver the kiss
and flick the switch off with her quick hand.
She never knew how torn I was
by those obliterating good nights.

As her lips touched my forehead
I looked sideways at the wagon train lampshade,
searching for the next moment
in the brilliant ambush, wondering
whose side I could ever be on.

Parting

From forehead to crown
the comb is dragged along your scalp
lengthways like a knife,

the large end tooth
making a pale furrow,
a white line of exposed skin.

Your mother presses
firmly enough to separate
one wing of hair from the other.

You are allowed to wince
but not flinch.
You must stand at attention

while the true mark
of parental care is drawn
right across the top of your mind.

River Ferry

He always made the most of that short voyage.
The ferry hauled itself across on chains
that rose dripping from the dark water.
I sat beside him in the helpless car.

He did Paul Robeson singing Shenandoah.
He called me Captain in his sternest voice,
his hand saluting crisply, with a quiver.
I played the game, but I only half laughed.

Riding a piece of roadway broken loose,
the current skidding in a slow sprawl
that kept on being fed from somewhere deep,
I couldn't see the journey as a joke.

At night I watched the shore lights shifting
as they came nearer, streets and houses lit
like close constellations, shaky stars
clearing the horizon of the dashboard.

My favourite moment was the quiet arrival.
The ferry stopped its awkward shuddering,
locked itself to the river bank, and then
my father suddenly became my father.

He bumped the gear stick into loose neutral
with the quick and casual seriousness I knew.
His hands went lightly to the steering wheel.
He was getting ready for the real road home.

Near Misses and Nothing

1. A clip over the ears

I remember the flash
of my grandfather's hand.
He'd launch a top spin drive

up and across the back of my head,
so close it ruffled hair
combed in honour of his visit.

This was his grandson greeting.
The mock ferocity, the fake swipe
missing by half an inch.

Its pin-point inaccuracy
made my day.
I stood in the small crowd of my family,

singled out
by the cloak of air thrown over me,
the hood of his hand.

2. Fishing

His cigarette did red hot loops
in the dusk, a scribble
with an instant fade.

When I asked him to do it again
he leaned into it
and wrote: *fish*.

I saw it hang and vanish.
For the split second
that longhand lived

no wind
could blow it away.
Though we reeled in

nothing,
I knew my grandfather's art.
Even the river went quiet

when he hauled off
and scrawled
his fiery weightless words.

Billycarting on Gravel

Get your best friend to give you his best push.
Streamline your young self by leaning forward,
hands at the ankles, chin behind the knees.
Keep the rope rein short and hold it hard.
At first you'll rattle down that unmade road,
but if the slope is long and steep enough,
trust me, at top speed you'll start to float.
Your front wheel spokes will gradually dissolve
and turn into a half transparent shimmer.
The loose surface beneath you will let go.
Airborne by no more than a millimetre,
this will be the moment that you live for,
lifted by a hint of weightlessness,
briefly adrift amongst the dust and stones.

The Dink

You rode sideways.
He reached around you to steer.
He'd given you his big brother groan

but he hadn't said no.
So there you were,
hanging on to the handlebars,

side-swiped by a freewheeling breeze,
going somewhere
in his incidental embrace.

You were his eternal
smaller passenger.
Your feet barely reached the pedals

but you dreamed of returning the favour.
You imagined
that huge struggling hug.

For now,
when he steadied the bike
and you hopped up backwards

it was always the ride of your life.
Held in the loose cage
of his arms,

you sat side-on
to every destination.
His headwind your crosswind.

The Weaving Mill

Half way to school, the saw tooth factory
shook with a sound like the crowded roar of surf.
The building seemed to hold a breaking sea.
Those waves crashed, and I lived to learn.

I crouched at my desk in the packed classroom.
I saw whole countries hanging from the wall
and Teacher striding his low platform.
He turned a watching back upon us all

to write his slanted lines of perfect longhand.
I watched them unfurl as he inched sideways,
chains woven of chalk, waves of a kind.
Words flowed from his fingers in whispers.

Everything vanished under the duster's hush,
but even the blackboard was a sky which went
with what the morning gave: the crash
of hidden ocean, the beach of the world it meant.

Going Dead

1

The game demanded tragic staggering,
slow motion falls on the front lawn.

Knees buckled, silver pistols
somersaulted out of our hands,

we sagged against weatherboards.
Nothing we loved so much as being killed.

Not that it occurred to us to die forever.
Death was the short-lived darkness

simmering behind our closed eyes,
the coolness of grass against our faces.

Hit in the heart, we lay there
suffering a momentary stillness,

ready to be reborn. We counted down
to each awakening. I can still see

my brother half collapsing on the run,
almost crawling in the end,

heading for another resurrection,
winning with the day's best death.

2

This is for the friend who wouldn't go dead.
Pleading imaginary trees, boulders

sprouting astoundingly in front of him,
he didn't want the joy of getting shot,

the pitching forward and lying there
with the sky's weight pinning you down,

your six-shooter useless beside you.
He kept whole landscapes up his sleeve.

Intangible cactus gave him cover,
canyons appeared out of nowhere.

We couldn't wipe the smile from his face.
When we stopped inviting him

his phantom props persisted. Unseen
stands of greenery crowded the lawn.

The corner where he had crouched
grinning behind transparent stone

teased us for weeks. His refusal to die
haunted that lawn. Its forgiving grass

was strewn with see-through trees,
ghost rocks the height of a boy.

3

The two girls two doors up
never went dead. We fired at them

and they laughed. Through loose fencing
we saw them ride their father's saw-horses,

feet stuck in stirrups made from stockings,
knees gripping the lucky timber.

I was in love with them so much
I hated them. They didn't kill each other.

They shot vaguely with their girls' guns.
At the end of a shoot-out they'd swing

one skinny leg over, dismount
and run to the clothesline post

on which they'd sketched Cheyenne
in chalk, and rescue him with kisses.

They smudged Clint Walker's smile
but he kept smiling. I was ten years old

and jealous of a post, its weathered
wood grain body and its drawn face,

those chalked chiselled features.
Once, I raided their alien world,

that death-free yard, and rubbed him out
with my bandana hanky. I rode off

on my invisible real horse,
slapping myself on the hip for speed.

But they brought Clint back with their mix
of chalk and love. I climbed the splintered

palings to see, and there he was, his lean
straight stance, his unkillable kissed smirk.

4
The day the tree removers moved in
we found our favourite side street

deep in wreckage, the highest limbs
brought down to earth for us to play amongst,

bunkers and trenches of greenery.
We prowled the parapets of felled growth,

picking each other off in caves of shade,
sniping from ground-level tree-tops.

Next afternoon it had all vanished.
A brand new sky was there to meet us.

With our hiding places harvested
and trucked away behind our backs,

we scouted for the still green scraps
the sweeper missed. We collected

bunches of leaves, held them in our fists
and raised our arms, pretending to be the trees,

who must have seen time running out for years,
the way they stood there with their hands up,

dropping everything at the command of autumn,
sneaking everything back each spring.

5
Until the elephant interrupted
we'd hardly noticed the circus over the road,

a tent city getting its act together.
The turbaned keeper came looking for water,

steering his huge pet up the driveway.
We stopped playing cowboys and Indians

the moment it swayed through the gate.
It hooked its trunk to a tap. When it left,

straying massively off the pavement only once,
our game reclaimed its territory.

But part of it was marked with hoof prints,
depressions the size of dinner plates,

the tough couch grass bent to the roots.
I recovered quickly from a confusion

of Indians, but I couldn't stop wondering
how one life could weigh so much.

We were almost weightless in ours.
We'd sprint across that lawn and leave no trace.

No matter how hard we threw ourselves down
in our dying, no imprint remained of us at all.

6
The closest we came to paradise
was taking potshots from the tree house

with live ammunition: rotten apples
grabbed from the bucket of windfalls

stacked in our branch-anchored fort.
Who needed bullets when you could hit

the Henderson boy in the heart with pulp?
He ran past us, pelting uselessly upwards,

while we were angels of ripe death
sending down fatal shirt stains.

We spent a night in that wind-shifted heaven.
Safe with the rope ladder hauled in,

keeping an eye on the real heavens
through the restless holes in our cloud

of leaves, we took aim at stray stars.
They flickered as if returning fire.

Back on the ground next morning,
practising the art of dying,

I hurled myself onto the lawn
at full speed. I lay on that thick grass,

eyes closed, my mind still running hard,
and felt a movement in everything,

a swaying that could have been
the branches of the earth holding me up.

2

Finding the Falls

Deep in the cold gorge
we're getting warmer.
River fall-out
carries past us,
towers of sunlight and spray,
skyscraper ghosts.
Additional shimmer
catches the trees.
The steep track shines.
Then there's the river
crashing into its pool,
unleashing its squalls.
We mime a shivery wonder,
we are frosted
with waterfall breath.
We manage a chilled kiss.
We have been drawn
to this staggering roar
of release, this storm
lost in the bush.
We have seen a whole river
let go, loosen
into lacy weightlessness,
shreds of its old self.
Now we stand
at its shuddering heart,
wrapped in a cannoning mist.
River atoms
fall all over us.

Dialogue after the Storm

The sky is a non-event.
The last squall is a fading fingerprint

on the horizon. I'll miss you,
your hunger for rain and time,

our shared passion for shelter.
We hoarded days

as if they were the answer.
I remember a downpour on the beach,

its roughness falling all over us.
The ocean was a wall so high

it lay down for us
and still we couldn't see over it.

An undertow of happiness hauled at me.
I wanted to drown

in the hours we spent together.
Every minute was a delicious dead end.

But here I am in the open-endedness
of an aftermath, the walls of a storm

vanishing into thin air,
the final fences of cloud dissolving.

The future is a vague version
of the past. With you

there was no such thing as too little time.
If I look straight at the sun

it becomes a cul-de-sac of light.
Your presence closes in.

*

Storms are in the eye of the beholder.
I remember a deluge of heat,

the sun devouring me
on that backwater beach.

I paid for it with peeling shoulders.
I can still feel you harvesting my skin,

flakes of me
in the palm of your hand.

I have had more than my fingers burned.
I have escaped the storm

in your eyes, your mind.
Once, time earned its keep

when the sea fog threw a blanket over us
and we were stranded

on a beach inside a cloud.
Or the night we woke to heat lightning,

a rapid-fire series of failed dawns
dragging us up the dunes

to watch the horizon turning itself inside out.
But so many moments led nowhere.

There were days when the future was a trap,
the world shrank

to one room
and I lived on a scrap of sky.

Promises can narrow down to nothing.
If the sun is a feast

and the rain is a festival,
you'll have to go alone.

Estuary

It was the half place we half loved.
A road disappearing beneath shallow sand,
a river almost becoming the sea.

We could take or leave
that vague harbour,
a destination that really wasn't one.

Even the hotel was half-hearted.
A twin room and the bar shut,
low level views of grass and marsh.

Sometimes an onshore wind
brought the sound of breakers,
as if a whole other story could be told.

But we were happy enough
with the incomplete silence of the estuary.
Those slightly inland nights

were all we needed.
We were lovers from elsewhere
making the best of a beach-free world,

an inlet quietness.
The beds we pushed together
never told a soul.

The Lighthouse

We abandoned the beach and the low dunes,
climbed a loose coastal path
and discovered the privacy of height.

Stunted scrub leaned away from a wind
coming off the ocean like an ocean.
The keeper's cottage was a clifftop wreck.

We lay down in the shade of the lighthouse.
We made a bed of the wind-whipped grass,
finding seclusion where there was no shelter.

At the foot of a locked pillar we were at home.
The cliff's edge was our private horizon.
The sea was present as an intense whisper.

The sun hunted us, but we were saved
by the beam of shadow from the lighthouse.
We left before we were outflanked.

Did they build these stone towers
to rescue lovers from the worst of summer?
We were taken under the wing

of a tall and uninhabited house.
We who found refuge in each other
left ourselves open to the sky.

Jealousy

1
The dunes are simmering.
Sand swarms across the beach at ankle height.
I tell you

it all remembers you.
This daybreak darkness,
the obsessive surf,

our old future.
If you have a promise to keep
be sure it isn't broken first.

*

You came back from these corners of the sea,
these angles of land,
a born mermaid.

I tasted the salt on your lips,
peeled the scales from your shoulders.
Your sun-blasted innocence convinced me.

I should have seen
the night sky in your eyes.
I should have looked for moonburn.

*

The sea keeps beaching itself,
sliding big sentences up the slope
in a hissed scrawl.

It knows something.
It won't stop
giving me its overlapping hints,

its sprawling news.
The oceanic script
sizzles and fades.

*

Tell me about that rogue summer,
you and your perfect stranger
making a home of this loose shore.

I want traces
of the pressure you put on each other,
signs of your settling in.

I am looking for what's left
of the shadows of clothing,
the remains of your whispers.

2
Tell me
the story.
Lean on your elbow
and let me have it, your slanted narrative.

How everything
turned on almost nothing,
a beach cliché.
The white noise of ocean.

Then something about the bravery of strangers
losing themselves in each other's lives.
How we take to betrayal.
I wonder if truth

is always like this,
the brand new thing that's been happening forever.
The flash of surf at night.
Being this close

while sleep threatens,
the decades intervene
and your story
wraps itself around me in the dark.

Istán and Other Places

Tell me which distant winter
you've infiltrated now. I'll pin

a frostbitten fragment of map
to my wall, a blown up overview

of some blizzard-riddled city. I'll imagine
parachuting in to track you down.

Finding you wrapped in your own arms
for warmth, I'd wade through foreign snow

to plead: Let me do that for you. We'd ignore
the flakes of white disintegrating sky

arresting us, all those weightless hands
coming to a soft stop on our shoulders.

But I have no chart of your unseasonable
drifting over borders. I will never land

feet first in alien terrain, gather in my wing
of strung silk, and set out after you.

I'm in the kitchen, squinting into a dusk
I know so well it seems to bloom

like a big vague shrub in my back yard.
It darkens in a daily autumn,

its infinitely small leaves of air
turning a deeper shade as evening falls.

Waiting out the aftermath
of your departure, I find this nearness

enough. I can make do with the night
presenting itself for inspection,

the moon clambering over the hedge,
my unclipped close horizon,

fog standing at the front fence,
proving that distance is disappearance.

Come back, surrender your passport.
It won't be needed in the underground

movement I'll enlist you in. We'll smuggle
warmth into a cold bed, defeat our secret

policing of the past. Already
I can see the routine morning siege.

Sunlight hugs the red brick wall
beside our window, flattening itself

to slide in and sprawl across the floor
when we pull the curtains back. The day

surrounds the house with time and light,
knowing we're in there. Calling us out.

*

Think of our wilderness trip,
the river with its overhangs,

its worn canyons. Rapids
like trenches of trapped surf,

outposts of ocean. And the sheen
of almost stationary deep water

creased by undercurrents,
stitches pulling the wrong way.

We slept on narrow beaches,
the river sprawling beside us.

Remember the last morning,
our tough pumped up raft

gatecrashing a pool between cliffs,
drifting out across a swirl

of water. We entered a ballroom
hung with rock, a strip of sky

for a streamer, the dance floor
slowly dancing with itself.

How much of this do you remember?
Maybe you live so vividly

the past is a lost cause.
Maybe each of your journeys buries

the one before. As for me
my whole enclosed life could rest

in that room the river led us to.
I'd set up a floating camp

and tempt you with a home
all space and movement,

an absent ceiling, a floor
of water sliding under us.

No handholds, no safe moorings.
You with your unanchored future,

me with somewhere to live
on the river's mirror skin.

*

There are interesting distances
at the front door. The road

gives me my dose of mirage,
little unreadable shimmers

in the midday heat, and further out
there's an almost legible

scattering of trees on a ridge-line.
A high altitude scrawl of cloud

is making the sky lean to one side.
Yesterday I watched a squall evaporate

as it trekked away across paddocks,
a fading curve of rain

on its last legs. My small portion of storm.
And closer to hand, the usual

inscrutable snapshots of you
confront me, placards of restlessness.

They picket my life with their icy
unidentifiable locations. In the latest

you're so far north the Aurora
unfolds above you, a scarf of light.

Longing never unlocks anything.
Keep sending me the photographs.

I won't demand names
for the far from innocent distances

surrounding you. I'll have to imagine
seeking you out, finding signs

only locals can read, learning
the language of frozen slopes

and low skies. I want to live
in the white-out background

to your tilted smile. I want to be there
when the blizzard comes

and all my inconclusive images of you
lose themselves in that blurred future.

*

Where are you now in the inexplicable
republics, those satellite dependencies

with their cold check points
further north than anywhere I've been.

I see you walking the stormed streets,
the wrecked squares. A mist

of tear gas, the whiff of history
stinging your eyes. I've seen the cars

in their stalled races, flames
waving like ecstatic passengers,

buildings torn open, frozen stage sets
exposed to the applause of war.

You and your addictive destinations.
I've had mine. One obsessive summer

I hiked the brittle Sierra Blanca.
The trail cut through limestone slopes

split by crevices, man-sized gaps
opening into miles of rock.

Those mountains were threaded
with space, laced with emptiness.

I kept to the track, its frayed curves
holding together all the way

to the end of itself at Istán.
The town was a blaze of whitewash.

People were dark shapes in the merciful
coolness of shops. A man who spoke

from a gauze patch on his throat
gave me a blood orange.

How many untranslatable nights
have you spent in your shaken cities?

You've taken the back roads across plains
flattened by war. Entire armies

have been ploughed under like stubble
in those raked fields. And there you are

stumbling out into a battered dusk
just in time to beat some lethal curfew.

Privacy can be subversive. You've evaded
safety, I've survived its dangers,

a map of the past my guide, memory
my weapon. If you were here

I'd show you the intensities
of going nowhere. The simmering wind,

the sea swarming closer on a clear night.
An attic with sky streaming in

at the window, verandahs with their protected
perspectives on everything.

We'd sit back and let the future
make its approaches. We'd track the past,

its besieging presence, its persistent
infiltrations. And if I have to settle for

sporadic correspondence, random
accounts of your far-flung life,

all I can offer in return are images
of refuge, memories of welcome.

Think of the honeycombed cliffs
of Istán, the man with the veiled voice

and the world inside the mountains,
networks of air, places carved out by rain

the earth has taken in for shelter.
Caverns reached by neither war nor winter.

The Giants of Barcelona

They floated around a corner,
heads level with the first floor window sills.
People waved at their painted eyes.

Their crowns were immense, their scarves
had huge folds. We were tourists
ambushed by this towering couple,

calmness and courtesy a storey high.
With a slight lean, they bowed.
They began their slow swirling dance.

We never discovered their names.
Living in the low-ceilinged room
of our new life, we spoke to almost no-one

in that maze of streets. But we knew,
looking up at those big faces,
how good it was to be dwarfed by them.

Something in our human smallness woke.
Propped in a doorway, we half embraced,
half leaned against each other.

They moved off, and we were left
in the backwash of their serenity.
We made our way through the festival,

the wake of those vast figures
eddying around us. The night breeze
was the wind from their robes.

Footage

Redwoods drift sideways and disappear,
moving out of frame as I zoom in.
Their lateral retreat reveals a curve
of trail, and you walking away from me.
A big tree intervenes on the next bend,
its massive forked flank gliding into view
at close range. Without a backward look
you're lost to sight behind its dark bulk.
Vision fades completely. Then there's forest
tilting and shuddering until I catch you
so far up ahead you're just a vivid
splinter of movement in the shaky distance.
The big trees stand around you like a downpour.
When you vanish this time there's no finding you.

Salt Fog

Inland, the town we started from recedes,
taking its lake with it, turning itself
into memory. The coastline we have come to
opens out, an expanse of destinations,

a thousand departure points. Even the fog
standing out to sea for hours this morning
offers something, the mystery of distance
seeing if an ocean takes its weight.

Short-term tourists, we are quickly addicted
to such a world. We can feel its strangeness
deepen around us as we drive north
on this narrow coastal road. The famous

forests begin to thicken, old growth walls
facing the sea mist. They are fed by it.
It comes ashore like the risen ghost
of the Pacific, leaving the faint taste of salt

on everything. For now, it's a rogue cloudbank
held at bay, as if the trees resist
what they thirst for, keeping it anchored
off the headlands. We see it from beached

stretches of highway. Hunting for hotels,
those small imagined havens further on,
we hope the redwoods hold out. We want the road
visible, the townships unencumbered

by a noon dusk. Time enough tonight
for the closing in, barricades of mist
making every street a false dead end,
the highway an endless cul-de-sac.

By then we'll have negotiated real
endings to the day. Adrift in sleep,
we'll casually invade each other's space
and half know it. No more need to imagine

arrival, an inexpensive room's warmth.
Outside, the all-embracing salt fog
will have flooded in. The big trees will be swamped
at last, the coast engulfed as it must be.

Velcro

that rasp
of separation

little connected hooks
pulling away from each other

that rich sound
of being torn apart

the best thing about
being so close

Saving Things

You could try lying sideways
and telling the truth straight
so your story wasn't coming at me from such an odd angle.

Maybe I'd stand for it maybe I'd take it lying down
so just how close we were
and whether we could face each other

would matter less than not having our backs to the wall.
With so much hanging over your head
I wouldn't want you to get yourself into a tight corner.

You won't need to jump through hoops to solve this.
You don't have to tread softly,
I'm not going to pull the rug from under you.

You say you'd do cartwheels for me
but I'm in the dark
and I really don't know where you're coming from.

Freeze

Did I dream that the trees bloomed in winter,
trying to retrieve the season?
The river froze because it wanted to go back.

We walked across a paralysed flow,
skirting hillocks of bunched-up ice.
The stressed landscape groaned.

Maybe beneath us the hidden river
went into reverse, maybe the fallen snow
lifted off and buried itself in the clouds.

I know time turned around for us.
The nights treated us as new lovers
though frost flowered on the leafless trees

and you were with me in the secrecy of sleep
like a shadow I knew better than myself.
Was this the past or future hauling at us?

Once, we found bridges superfluous.
I watched as you walked on the roof of a river.
We surrendered to the undertow of days.

Memory can be a river going the wrong way.
To keep faith with the life we've led
think of that winter as waiting for us.

3

Finding Poetry

Go to the bravest shelves.
Let your fingers climb the alphabetical cliffs.
Put your head on sideways to read the narrow titles.

Bend backwards and reach up
for something from a foreign language.
Reader, contortionist,

who knows what shape you'll be in
when you have bent in half for the lower poets.
How will you get through the day

with this rearranged version of yourself.
Your upside-down mind,
your translated heart.

Destinations

They do strange things.

They surround us and let us go.
They are born again backwards
in the rear vision mirror.

Some are never found.

Remember the dark end of the street
in that song about midnight love?

And miles to the north of this highway
sunlight is pouring down
through a break in the clouds.

But the road is taking us west
and fast.
The unlit street and the lost storm of light
are behind us already.

Late in the day
the sun will hit the earth ahead of us
and bury itself before we can get to it.

Let's drive through the night
with the radio on.
Let's hunt for destination songs.

If that midnight street appears
this time we'll go there.

Windy Night, with Clouds

Don't look up.
Creation is making a dash for it.

The moon and stars are speeding in the same direction,
dragging the sky with them.

Down here
the tree tops are under way,
sagging and straightening,
trailing after the escaping constellations.
The ground races
and the grass goes with it, hanging on by its roots.

The whole earth streams
towards a huge horizon.

Only the clouds,
those strange anchors,
are staying put.

When the moon hits them
they are suddenly see-through.
And look, there is more to them than weightless frailty.

Packed with dark possibilities of rain,
they are something to hold on to on a night like this.

They are standing by
for the next time a world comes around.

Insomniac

I have sleep beaten.
I have the night in a tight corner.

Nothing can catch me napping,
falling asleep,
sleeping through,
drifting off,
sleeping in.

I'm your expert
on the textures of the dark,
the pressure rain puts on a room,
thunder distances.

Tonight
a downpour trashed the street in a 4am fury,
a small hour squall.

Now there's the usual
tricky quietness.
The wind is loosening fistfuls of rain
from the trees.
They are hitting the roof
in that heavy, hesitant way.

The storm's afterthoughts,
a sleep trap.

Too little,
too late.

I've heard the night unleash itself.
I know how it thrashes around,
looking for a way out of its own darkness.

The stars and moon
which are probably shining now
are its stopgap measures.

The dawn is its desperate invention.

Death of a Dragonfly

So many of your peers veered away
at the last moment,
missing the sloped windscreen,
riding the car-shaped cushion of air
to safety of a kind.
They vanished at freeway speed.
You alone
snagged on the aerial,
an instant banner
of bad luck.
I couldn't believe
you were hanging on,
your long tough body bent and caught,
your gauze wings intact.
They shuddered and streamed,
leaves of gold lace
open to everything the world was hurling at them.
I didn't slow down.
I might have loosened
your oblivious grip.
I wanted to make it all the way home
with the radio on
and your wings
picking up the lace frequencies,
the gauze wavelengths,
the smallest songs.

The Dispersal

I know now
what it was, that airborne spindrift,
that distorted snowfall.

I have studied
the migration of spiders,
how they fish for the wind with silk

and lift off.
How swarms of them sail for miles.
But their blizzard

baffled me when it happened.
A hairline shimmer crowded the sky.
Nature strips glinted,

fences were glistening hedges.
Twists of web
surged on the breeze.

I never suspected a spiderling storm.
I would have searched for them,
tiny passengers,

invisible hangers on,
But all I saw were skeins of weightlessness,
air maps on the move.

The Runaway God

1
In the small hours
he left,
decided to pocket the moon.

Revenge,
that cold light
slapping against his thigh
while he ran
the back streets of the universe.

2
Free of moon pull,
wholly human at last,
only the werewolves approved.

Lovers mourned the tides of the heart.

3
Let them eat starlight

was his last thought
as he crossed the borders of creation.

The Ballad of Narcissus

The blood on your brow was claret,
your umbilical cord was silk.
The very first words you uttered
were Waiter, bring me my milk.

Now time is nothing but trouble,
time is a teller of lies.
At twenty you were so lovely
you couldn't believe your eyes.

Your flesh was Swedish crystal,
your bones were Venetian glass.
When you stood in front of the mirror
miracles came to pass.

But you met your terrible fate
as so many lovers must.
In a moment of confusion
the dream turned into dust.

The bar was badly lit,
there were mirrors on the wall,
and you caught a winning smile
from the fairest of them all.

No one yelled a warning,
no one had a chance.
No one could have known
you'd ask yourself to dance.

A glamorous collision
and suddenly nothing there
but a scintillating haze,
a ringing in the air.

Wet Evening

(after the painting by Clarice Beckett)

To make the world like this
and keep it that way, with only the dusk

blackening roadside trees, the washed road
reflecting the coolest of skies

and that patch of flame colour
nothing to worry about, maybe

a street lamp. This would be a creation
worth the creator's restraint.

Not to be tempted by summer,
its gale force blue and tinder distances,

its withering brilliance. To know that the blur
of rain is a sure sign of salvation,

that a shimmer of light on bitumen
is all we need to mark our passing.

This is the knowledge we want
in a maker. Whoever is in the van

with its huge warm tail-light
is safe, steering towards the next

mysterious bend, heading for home
through the unburnt world.

Drifting Clouds

(after the painting by W. B. McInnes)

Forgive me, but this cloudscape isn't drifting.
Not if we mean by that a weightless shifting

sideways on some innocent slight breeze.
Descending with a vengeance is what these

storm weighted clouds are doing. Note the dark
pressure bearing down in them, the stark

threat to a straightforward working paddock scene.
Think of McInnes, how it must have been,

preparing his rough pastoral, to find
an avalanche of weather on his mind.

At least he finished here, everything stopped
short of obliteration, those clouds propped,

the background houses and the foreground cattle
just saved from being victims in the battle

waged with this squall of paint: how to prevent
it wiping out a sunlit world it's meant

simply to shadow briefly and proceed.
Why wouldn't we, imagining the need

to find a name that's safe to know it by,
forgive him for being frightened of his sky.

The Trestle Dance

They have come down from the hills
and have erected their long tables
on the river flats. They bring no music
but the slam of boots on wood,
the women with weighted skirts
and the men with jackets buttoned
to the neck. It's a half march,
half reel, a combination stomp
and whirl, and with every dance
the trestles press deeper
into the soil. The broad-brimmed
hats of the men stay strictly level,
the women's hair flares and settles
as they crash and glide. No dancer
watches another, no one
says a word. They were born
to the sequences. They are packed
together in a perfect blur
of bodies. As darkness falls
they seem to be hovering, a mass dance
a few feet off the ground, their crashing
sweep a kind of floating. They blend
into each other and the coming night.
Down the valley, the sound
blooms in the wind, the locals
half remembering old stories
and half wondering about thunder,
the storm that never reaches them.

Bridge

for the men of the West Gate, 1970

It's a long useless roof,
a failed shelter
for an acre of estuary,
so the rain
blows in from the bay in vague ribbons
and reaches everything,
takes the shine off the water between piers,
adds a contradictory sheen
to the vacant pavement of the walking trail
and applies a gloss
to the engraved plaque,
a bronze cliff
covered with names,
the chiselled words collecting run-off,
a cold gleam
in each incised stroke,
every unprotected letter
harbouring a trace of squall.

*

The torn angel of the bridge
flourishes its wing,
a big flag flying alone,
the missing wing lost
when the concrete sky fell
and the angel flew under it
to be with the trapped men
and a trailing wing was pinned
by the rogue span,
its caught force
dissolving with the unsaved lives,

vanishing into ground
the angel never leaves now,
for the healed bridge
needs the damaged angel,
whose single wing
flares invisibly everywhere,
a flung cape
of light by day
and darkness by night,
strengthening the fabric of the air,
keeping the bridge whole,
the sky in its place.

*

Seen from beneath it's on the move,
its high outline
gliding beneath clouds,
as if the cable-stayed structure is free
of its famous foundations
and the collapse upwards
the unrecovered dead were dreaming of
is happening at last,
the buried bedrock ties broken
as the bridge turns wing
and the stressed spans lift off,
inner urban mudflats torn apart,
the safe sweep of river
flecked with momentary rapids,
swirls of silt flowering
and settling back,
abandoned by a departing bridge,
its traffic about to be carried elsewhere for ever
while the irretrievable workers,
released from the tidal reaches,
climb aboard,
knowing there's time

to find a foothold and hang on,
waving their hard hats hard at all of us,
loving the looks on faces they will never see,
the forgiven bridge shaking the earth from its feet.

*

Strange how a blinding version of the day
waits for us on some bend
or over this rise
as the late sun fires up reflections
on what could well be rooftops,
maybe lakes
scattered across the peak hour urban sprawl
when we crest the West Gate,
sky fallen to its knees in white hot cloud
and rich industrial air
putting a wash of manufactured haze
over the suburbs,
layers of mirage
recreating the old distances at altitude,
a frail history risen,
insubstantial fields of blurred half-landscape,
outer reaches of the loved city,
remembered grasslands
riding a storm of oil refineries,
the intermittent scrub adrift
and this freeway,
sideswiped by radiance as it gains height,
floats under us,
an airborne road,
its traffic shimmering,
the lanes alive with weightlessness,
our way home disconnected from the earth.

River Lines

A river
runs through this poem.

River images
are piling up.

Cauldrons
of worn rock.
Drowned landslips.
Stationary waves
swaying as they stay put.

The river swerves against the slopes
of the poem.
River distances
appear out of nowhere.
Mountains,
a narrow sky.

Then cliffs
and dark pools.
Undercurrents and eddies.

The river has settled in.

But the poem is beginning to wonder
about the river.

The way it mutters to itself.

Its inescapable weight.

Its endless
arrival.

*

There was too much river in the poem.

Reading it
was wall to wall river.

There was no way out
of the poem's flooded ravines,
no way of telling
poem from river.
Words whispering
as they swept around a bend,
all that print
moving on to downstream meanings.

The river overflowed the poem
and escaped.

For a while
there were hints of river.
The occasional gleaming line,
a river word or two
glinting in the distance.

Now the poem
has no river in it.
It doesn't know where the river is.
It remembers the river
and talks about it.

Although it knows better
the poem wants to be the river.

*

The river has gone.

The poem is all sky
and mountain.

It wants the river rewritten.

But the river will not return.
It's free
to be pursued
by thoughts that have never occurred to anyone.
It has shaken off
the known mind.

It flows
somewhere on the other side of everything.

It's searching
for new mountains.
A sky.

It remains
the unwritten river.

*

The river lives
on the other side of everything.
It's beyond the reach of the poem.

The poem thinks of the river
as a shining rope.
The river
ties a mountain
to the earth.

Sky is tethered to the top of the mountain
by a slipstream
of cloud.

The poem admits
it is making this up.

It wants to fill
the river void.

But the hidden river insists.

It has found unimaginable mountains,
unwritable sky.

Climate Change

is so huge
I mean the Garnaut Report
with its billion words
barely scratched the surface,
showed us only the tip of the iceberg
(for those of you who may be reading this
in another century, icebergs
were enormous floating fragments of the famous
polar ice-caps), and my poem
was going to be a saga, a verse monster
the size of the Encyclopaedia Brittanica
(for those who may be reading this
in another century, this was a book
as big as an iceberg, packed with frozen knowledge)
but I thought about the carbon footprint
of all that print, every letter an ant's breath
of greenhouse gas, and my laptop doing its bit
to heat up the world, not to mention the making
of the paper (what a hoofmark that would leave on the future).
So I stopped right here.

The Mirror Hurlers

in memory of Joyce Lee

1. The Looking-Glass Apprentice

Mistress, I saw the sunlight swim on red brick walls. Your mirror flew
from a high window. The crash hit backwater bedrooms, distant kitchens.

The frame had shattered but the uncracked mirror flashed, a pool
amongst ruins. Your voice flooded the laneway. "Try it. Mirror hurling

goes back centuries." I grab my full-length mirror, stagger to the window.
The mirror leans against me, a cape made of myself. Brick walls

move in the heat. I cart the mirror back to its dark corner, and you talk
of leaving. Mistress, I know you want real height, sky streaming in

at your front door, but show me survival again. Think of me here,
lanes like canyons around me. All my mirrors unhurled.

2. The Mirror

This is my sworn story of staying whole. For years I dreaded
slippery-fingered servants, but the mirror mistress held me
like a kept promise. When she threw me, I sailed through my cousin
the window, and the air whispered of weightlessness. Falling
was a new way of being held. The crash was a savage cradling.

Now my unbreakable shine waits for you all. Come to me
for the backhanded truth of who you are. See, your left hand
knows exactly what your right hand is doing. Your crooked smile
slants the other way. And notice the fake depth in your eyes, your thin
visiting presence. Stranger, I give you your shallow reversed self.

3. The Mirror Detective

I know them. Their two-faced ways, their almost invisible
shimmers of thought. They are thieves, stealing mirrors
and hurling them into the world. They won't get away with it.

I am after them, with my dull routine and my non-reflective mind.
I'll hunt them down. I'll climb the stairs, knock on the last door
and there it will all be: open windows, mirrors in mattresses,
tables littered with wrecked frames. Mirror hurlers at work.

They'll soon find out their mirror hurling days are over.
I'll let them know that prison mirrors are made of tin.
They will put on their long coats. I will frisk them for mirrors.

4. The Mirror Lovers

There are those who will never release their mirrors.
They cannot surrender their perfect self-portraits.
They sleep with them. They wake up beside themselves
in dim rooms, and wonder if they have married.

All day there's a quicksilver gleam in their eyes.
They feel strangely flat. They have to resist
an impulse to mime the movements of others.
Their minds are full of unwanted reflections.

At night, they return to the mimicry of marriage.
The fingertip touching, the two-dimensional tenderness.

5. The Mirror Mistress

I loved the lanes,
the early morning shudder of sun across old brick.

But here on this cliff top
with its mountains of pure space, I know I have come home.

Looking-glass lakes are scattered across the earth,
my run-up takes me

right to the edge.
I let the mirror go and everything seems to slide.

I am wiped from the mirror's mind.
I am replaced by sky.

Thirteen Ways of Thinking about a Chainsaw

1
It's a cross between a shark and a bicycle.

2
It can't swim
and it shouldn't be ridden.

3
Don't kick it.
Its kickback kills.

4
Trees go weak at the knees when they see one.

5
Plantation pines throw themselves to the ground
and splinter spontaneously into structural timber
the moment they hear the mutter of a chainsaw.

6
I knew a poet whose mind was a chainsaw.
When he attacked someone's poem
word dust flew into the air.
He's not been the same
since one of my syllables hit him in the eye.

7
When a chainsaw sinks its teeth into woodflesh
why does it pull you towards the cut?

8

If you see something snagged in the chain
don't reach forward to clear it.
You may have to wave your hand goodbye.

9

Never take a chainsaw out while drunk.
You might ask it to dance.

10

There are babies whose cry is remarkably like a chainsaw at full
throttle.
Their parents' minds have been turned to sawdust.

11

Why can't they make chainsaws
sound like lyrebirds?

12

Like your novel, chainsaws can be difficult to start.

13

Like your novel, maybe it would be best if chainsaws were
impossible to start.

Apology

I cannot make it. Hope it all goes well.
The life you plan to have looks interesting,
although I must admit it's hard to tell
these days, what with the world and everything.
There's a vague backwards drift beneath it all
and going well may not be all that easy.
One step forward, two back, backs to the wall
— going nowhere keeps us pretty busy.
But anyway, the years you've chosen seem
beyond me, like the fast retreating sky
I see this evening. Vapour cities stream
away, collapsing in a vast goodbye.
There's grey and silver wreckage in the blue.
There's everything and nothing left to do.

The Afternoon

It was a midday-triggered stretch of time.
It took us to the edge of that last evening,
the day's end coming at us like a squall
making for richer light on everything.

Remnants of the sea discovered us,
salt-encrusted mirror images.
Some were so deep and wide we swam in them,
pale enormous starfish treading water.

After we hit the soft embankment of dusk,
impossible to think we could forget
the promontory of hours on which we'd wandered.
Half of the sun's world given to us.

Instructions for the Day

Raise the sun
no matter what mess the clouds find themselves in.
This will get rid of the stars,
those itches of light.

Set people free from dreams
or the absence of dreams.
Give them their different horizons.
Some will be able to see the curve of the earth.
Some will see no further than the back fence.

Let warmth and light increase
until all shadows point south.
Undo the morning.
Declare the afternoon.

You are at your best then.
Each hour intensifies the sun's presence.
Homes hold light
and workers know the promise of release.
Shade spreads east
as if searching for the beginnings of all this.

Be aware: completion looms.
Allow yourself to fade gracefully.
Tolerate the early sleep of children,
the million glimpses of family life at dusk.

When you feel another batch of stars
surfacing through your skin of light,
let everything go.
Your world will dissolve.
Call it a day.

Flight Thoughts

The wings are getting the most out of thin air.

Sky is trying to enter through the head-shaped windows.

Some of us drift
in a double glazed sleep,
ears plugged,
both eyes patched.

Some of us are speed readers.
The words travel at a thousand kilometres an hour.

We live in a silver bullet
and are given everything.
Balanced meals,
survival skills,
oxygen ready to pounce.

For those with small egos
self-inflating life jackets are provided.

For lovers, a supervising moon.

At dawn, a new ocean inches towards us.
The horizon has printed out a continent.

There will be towns
where people wake to a clear day
and think of impossible thunder.

We travel ahead of the sound of our passing.
We are visible only as a vapour trail.

Buying Online

1
If the book arrives bent
put it down to the curve of the earth.

Money heads for the horizon and disappears.
It comes back
as poetry.

Such small amounts of money,
so many poems
responsive to the gravity of being in the world.

2
Our days are salt-stained.
They come to us from some hidden anchorage,
they have passed through the straits.

They are cargoes of time and light.
We are safe harbours for them.

Put everything on the line.
Risk your details,
trust your carrier,
order all the days you can afford.

3
There's the olive leaf concept,
the dove returning
with an image of the saved world.

It takes a whole branch to mean peace
but Noah was thankful for the immense small mercy.

How many love poems from the last century
does it take to save this one?
Send for them
and they fly in like fierce doves.

As for the raven who never returned,
who knows what poem he has become.

4
Remember the drowned poems.

Lost overboard
in the oceanic distances.

Wrecked in our famous gales.

Some washed up on the steep beaches
with their lifeless forms intact.

As they were buried
they were read.

All that truth legible at the edge of the grave.

5
Poetry can come by air,
trailing clouds of vapour.
Glory of a sort.

You pay more,
but the poems reach you at high speed
and their sound trails behind them.

Open the book,
pick a word
and brace yourself
for its full weight to land on you.

You will feel the breaking
of the meaning barrier.

6
Imagine a poem light years away,
moving at 186,000 miles per second.
It may take centuries to reach us.

If it has mass
the poem will be infinitely heavy.

We don't want it crashing into our minds
at the speed of light.
The weight of its words would be unbearable.

But the poem *is* light.
It will arrive
as a weightless wavelength of language.

None of us will live to read it.

It will threaten nothing.
It will change everything.

7
There's a stained poem.
Rain has damaged the book it belongs to.

The poem cannot be blamed for poor packaging
or rough handling,
but bad weather now needs to be read into it.

Dampness has reached up the page
and invaded the last stanza.
The poem's ending is underpinned by a vague warping.

Keep the book.
Forget a refund.
It's a bonus,
this poem open to the elements.

Think of the weather wanting to get to the poem,
the rain being interested enough.

8
If the book is badly bent
poems won't recover.

They will be haunted
by contortions.

They will never flatten.

They will be left with an undulation,
a lift in the lines
no one knows the meaning of.

9
These are spindrift words.
They hang back
from the main point.

They make the smallest possible impact.
They will come to nothing.
You can have them free of charge.

Feel their faint rain,
thoughts that fade as they hit you.

Acknowledgments

Poems and versions of poems in this collection have been published in *Meanjin, Antipodes, Poetry Monash, Landlines, Blue Dog, Going Down Swinging, Island, The Canberra Times, Australian Poetry Journal, Australian Poetry Anthology, Australian Book Review*, the Central Coast Poets 2012 anthology *Seeking the Sun*, the 2016 and 2018 Newcastle Poetry Prize anthologies and Inkerman and Blunt's *Australian Love Poems 2013*.

Individual poems have also been recognised in a range of awards, including: 'Near Misses and Nothing', first prize (under the title 'My Grandfather's Art') in the 2008 FAW John Shaw Nielson Award; 'Insomniac', first prize in the 2008 Woorilla Poetry Prize; an abridged version of 'Going Dead', second prize in the 2010 Val Vallis Poetry Award; 'River Lines' and 'Bridge', shortlisted for the Blake Poetry Prize in 2013 and 2014 respectively; 'Istán and Other Places' (an abridged version), second prize in the 2016 Newcastle Poetry Prize; 'Buying Online', first prize in the 2018 Newcastle Poetry Prize, and 'The Mirror Hurlers', shortlisted for the 2019 Peter Porter Poetry prize.

Major thanks to Nathan Curnow, Ross Donlon, Anne Gleeson and Lorraine McGuigan for such high quality input over the last ten years or more, and to my wife, Julie Phillips, whose wise presence and insights have accompanied me for almost the entirety of my poetry life. For their work as readers of this manuscript in its formative stages, I owe a great deal to Paul Croucher and Catherine de Saint Phalle, and Deb Shnookal provided invaluable technical support at a critical point.

I acknowledge with gratitude the assistance of a grant from the Literature Board of the Australia Council.

About the Author

Ross Gillett's poems have appeared in *The Age, The Australian* and *The Canberra Times* and in journals including *Meanjin, Quadrant, Overland, Poetry Monash, Island, Antipodes, Going Down Swinging, Blue Dog, Australian Poetry Journal* and *Australian Poetry Anthology*. They featured three times in Black Inc's *The Best Australian Poems*. His book *The Sea Factory* was one of the Five Islands Press New Poets 2006 series. In 2010 he published a chapbook of old and new poems – *Wundawax and other poems* - with Mark Time Books.

His awards include the Robert Harris Poetry Prize, the Broadway Poetry Prize, the Reason-Brisbane Poetry Prize, the City of Greater Dandenong National Poetry Prize and the Melbourne Poet's Union National Poetry Prize. Individual poems in this collection have won the Woorilla Poetry Prize, the FAW John Shaw Nielson Award and the Newcastle Poetry Prize. In 2019 Ross was shortlisted for the Peter Porter Poetry Prize and the Newcastle Poetry Prize.

He lives in Daylesford in the Central Highlands of Victoria.

www.ingramcontent.com/pod-product-compliance
Lightning Source LLC
Chambersburg PA
CBHW031002090426
42737CB00008B/644